MW00931709

candid

men

candid

/ Kandɪd /

Learn how to pronounce

adjective

1. 1 .

truthful and straightforward; Frank.

"his responses were remarkably candid"

synonyms:
frank , outspoken , forthright , blunt , open , honest ,
truthful , sincere , direct , straightforward , plain-spoken ,
bluff , unreserved , downright , not afraid to call a spade
a spade, straight from the shoulder, unvarnished , bald ;

1. 2 .

(of a photograph of a person) taken informally,
especially without the subject's knowledge.
"it is better to let the photographer mingle among the
guests and take candid shots"

synonyms:
unposed , informal , uncontrived , unstudied , impromptu
;

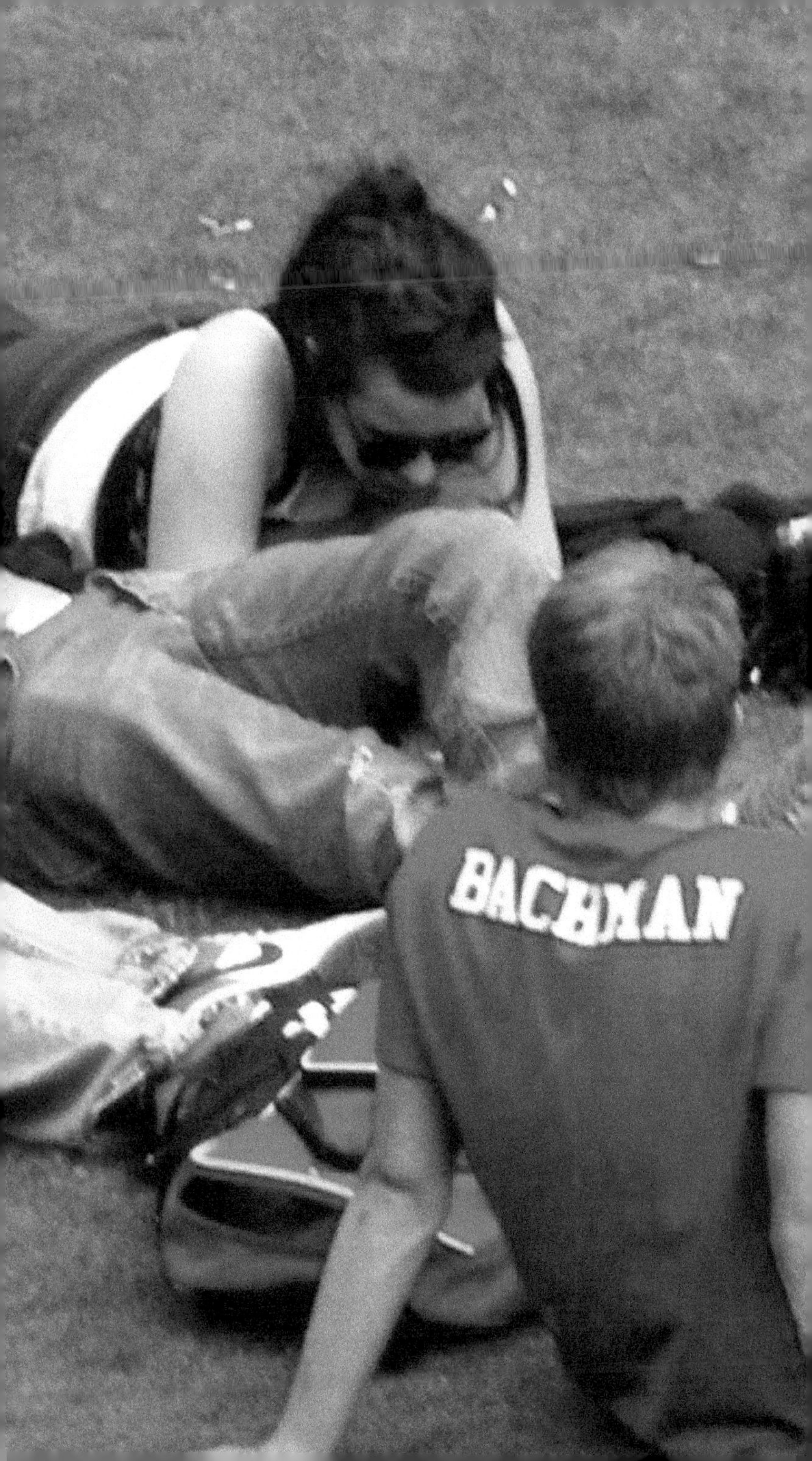
BACHMAN

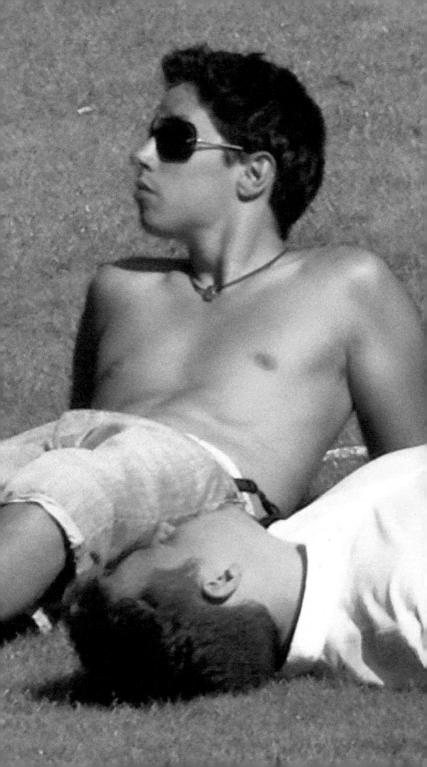

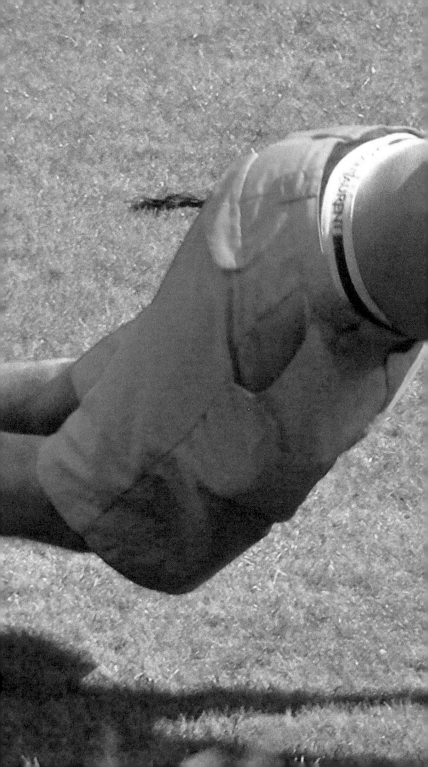

THE
GARDEN CAF

at the morning special
on a croissant

Cafetière Coffee

Freshly made sandwiches

Fresh Salads

Cakes & Biscuits

Soft Drinks

Wine & Beer

CPSIA information can be obtained
at www.ICGtesting.com
Printed in the USA
BVHW020928240719
554056BV00047B/1898/P

9 780464 048770